Skirmishes with
the Inland Revenue

Daniel Dover
and
Tim Hindle

with cartoons by
McLachlan

P

PROFILE BOOKS

First published in Great Britain in 2003 by
PROFILE BOOKS LTD
58A Hatton Garden
London ECIN 8LX
www.profilebooks.co.uk

Copyright © BDO Stoy Hayward 2003
8 Baker Street
London WIU 3LL
www.bdo.co.uk

Typeset in Columbus by MacGuru
info@macguru.org.uk

Printed in Great Britain by
Bookmarque, Croydon, Surrey

A CIP catalogue record for this book is available from the British Library.

ISBN 1 86197 524 4

Contents

Foreword

This book is designed to help anyone who is (or thinks they might be) the subject of an Inland Revenue enquiry into their tax affairs. It is not a detailed guide about what to do and when. It is a rough map of where you will be if you get into the territory of a Revenue enquiry. It can be dangerous territory for the uninitiated, particularly as it can lead on to an investigation.

Ten per cent of all Revenue enquiries today are said to be selected entirely at random. And each year there are over 250,000 enquiries in all. So some 25,000 people every year are selected for enquiry for absolutely no reason whatsoever. You could very easily be one of them.

Most enquiries are reasonably innocent affairs, but few of us feel entirely at ease about communicating with the Revenue. Some of us, of course, have due cause to feel uneasy. All of us need to know when it is safe to put our heads above the parapet, and when not. And we cannot do that without guidance. Whatever you do, don't skirmish seriously with the Revenue without decent intelligence – far more than is provided in this slim volume.

We are grateful to many people for their help in the production of this book. To Peter Leach, who was there at the conception; to Peter Fairchild, Frank Goldberg, Philip Spencer, Mike Sutherland and Andy Williams for their expert knowledge so patiently revealed; and to Marina Line for making it happen. Outside BDO Stoy Hayward, thanks are due to our wives, Helen and Ellian, who may occasionally have wondered why one little book required us to spend so many evenings together. Our children may never understand.

Lastly, a word of thanks to the main protagonists of this book: the Inland Revenue, without whom ...

Daniel Dover
Tim Hindle
December 2002

Introduction

When the Inland Revenue open an enquiry into a taxpayer's affairs, the experience is rarely pleasant. Even the totally innocent assume they are guilty. And they may well be guilty of having made a mistake. For the tax returns that over nine million UK taxpayers are now obliged to fill in every year are becoming increasingly complicated.

At the same time, the average British citizen's financial affairs are also more and more complicated. A larger number of people own shares than ever before, and more own property to rent. These give rise not only to a potential income-tax liability but also to the possibility of capital-gains tax, a much less straightforward affair, which also has to be recorded on tax returns.

Then again, more people work for themselves these days. They are self-employed instead of being on an employer's PAYE system, which more or less automatically calculates their income-tax liability for them.

In the years since the responsibility for filling in tax returns correctly was passed fairly and squarely to individual taxpayers, those returns have become more difficult to complete. In 1996/97, the first fiscal year of self-assessment, there were two supplementary pages for capital gains; now there are eight. If it seemed like a good idea to the Revenue in 1995 to shift responsibility to the taxpayer, it must seem like a stroke of genius today. The length of the forms, however, is proving counterproductive. So difficult are they to fill in that the Revenue are working on a simpler four-page specimen that they hope will be sufficient for the majority of taxpayers.

The self-assessment system frees up the Revenue to enquire more into taxpayers' returns. The Revenue have made it clear to all their staff that they do not have to have reasons to believe a return is incorrect before setting out on an enquiry. If the Venerable Bede were alive today, the saintly seventh-century monk could be the subject of an enquiry. The Revenue would not have to have reasonable suspicion that he was misbeehiving (under-reporting revenues from his honey business, for example, or trying to pass off habits as 'workwear') before asking him to answer a few searching questions. Even he might soon find himself in a sticky position.

Some suspect that the Revenue behave on occasions like a traffic warden with fixed targets to achieve. There seems no other obvious explanation for requests that go out to taxpayers asking them to do no more than resubmit things like their P60 forms – forms on which it is virtually impossible to make an accidental mistake.

On the whole, however, the Revenue's enquiries are becoming more targeted, more oriented towards those

> No battle ... takes place as those who planned it
> anticipated. That is an essential condition.
> A countless number of free forces ... influence
> the course taken by the fight, and that course never
> can be known in advance and never coincides with
> the direction of any one force.
>
> *Leo Tolstoy, War and Peace*

taxpayers who are likely to prove fruitful. These days, in the ongoing war between the taxman and the taxpayer, there is less of a scatter-gun approach, more of a series of carefully aimed shots.

And make no mistake. This is similar to a war, a battle in which taxpayers are prepared to use almost any weapon to hang on to their income and capital, while the Revenue fight back with low cunning and high technology to recapture what they consider to be their rightful share. When the Revenue open an enquiry, they engage in a close encounter with the taxpayer in which each side has a broad array of weapons available to it.

Such skirmishes with the Revenue occur all the time. Taxpayers produce evidence to show that they have paid

> Conscience is the inner voice that tells you the
> Revenue might check your tax return.
>
> *Anon*

their dues and should be allowed to go free. The Revenue then counter with, perhaps, a new interpretation of the law. But this can be a dangerous practice. Little skirmishes in relatively safe territory can easily escalate into damaging battles. Taxpayers need to be aware of the basic rules of engagement with the Revenue before they start. Or they need to seek advice from experts who know what the rules are. Only then can they learn how to avoid a war and win a peace that leaves them with as much of their property as possible. Of the two options – War or Peace – peace is preferable. Believe us.

The opening shots

An engagement with the Revenue can be said to begin when a taxpayer receives a letter informing him that he is the subject of an enquiry, and asking him to send further information to the Revenue. (Incidentally, taxpayers are female too, but for some curious non-sexist reason the majority of enquiries are into the affairs of men. So, throughout this book, we refer to taxpayers who are engaged in battle with the Revenue as male.)

This letter is the taxman's opening shot, and is known as a 'Mae West letter' because it promises that someone will come and see you sometime! Regrettably, only a few of the inspectors who do come and see you look anything like Mae West, although an increasing number of them are of the same gender.

A typical opening letter of enquiry is shown opposite. In general, the Revenue expect to receive replies to its correspondence within 28 working days.

Receiving notice of an enquiry by the Revenue has

Inland Revenue

Tel:
Ext:
Fax:

Area Director

Date
Our Ref:
Your Ref:

Help us to help you; when
telephoning or writing, please quote
our reference, and your surname and
National Insurance Number

Dear Sir

Thank you for your Tax Return for the year ended 5 April 200 . I am
writing to tell you that I intend to make some enquiries into this return.
I have written to your tax adviser, BDO Stoy Hayward, to ask for the
information I need.

I enclose a copy of our Code of Practice. It explains how we make
enquiries and how we keep our promise of fair treatment under the
Revenue's Service Commitment to you.

When you have read the leaflet, please contact me if you require further
information.

Yours faithfully

H M Inspector of Taxes

been compared to having an autopsy without the benefit of death. Some people go faint whenever they see so much as an envelope from the Revenue. When it eventually proves to contain a cheque for over-payment of tax, they are liable to go faint again. In this situation recovery is quick. But cases of severe after-shock have been known. Such is our instinctive feeling of guilt about our relationship with the taxman.

The experience can be even more traumatic when the taxpayer receives a general letter saying that the Revenue are opening an enquiry, but without giving any details. These, the letter explains with gut-wrenching suspense, have been sent separately to the taxpayer's adviser with a detailed request for information. The taxpayer can be left in a cold sweat for days until the second letter finally arrives at his adviser's office.

The Revenue have mercifully indicated that they are going to change this practice, and to start sending the same letter to both taxpayer and adviser at the same time.

One taxpayer found himself reading an advertisement for offshore tax advisers which boasted that if he were to invest with them he would never get a letter from the Revenue like the one that they were publishing in the advertisement. Funnily enough, he had got just such a letter that very morning.

Fear is increased under the self-assessment system because taxpayers who receive a letter from the Revenue informing them that they are the subject of an investigation do not know whether they are one of the minority selected entirely at random, or one of the majority, about whom the Revenue already have some grounds for suspicion.

But fear does not help in dealing with enquiries. Remember that, in practice, few enquiries end up with taxpayers paying fines or penalties, and even fewer end up with anyone going to jail.

Types of skirmish

The Revenue carry out two distinct types of enquiry:

1 'aspect' enquiries, and
2 general enquiries.

They do have internal targets of their own – to detect non-compliance in three out of every four enquiries that they carry out.

> One case which helped the Revenue to reach its target in 2001 was that of a bonsai-tree farmer who was subjected to a highly stressful three-year investigation. At the end of the enquiry he was told that he owed the Revenue the mighty sum of 22 pence. The inspector's bark was clearly worse than his bite.

In an aspect enquiry, the Revenue look at one or two particular aspects of a taxpayer's return. They may want to question a particular claim for expenses or some item of the taxpayer's overseas income. Most aspect enquiries are straightforward and do not merit the taxpayer employing a specialist adviser.

General enquiries are much more wide-ranging (and rarer). In such cases, the inspector wants to see absolutely everything – receipts and cheque stubs, for example, and even seemingly irrelevant documents like bank statements for non-interest-bearing accounts. General enquiries are most frequently aimed at the self-employed. Anyone subject to a full general enquiry is advised to seek professional help immediately. They will be in dire need of a briefing and some serious front-line intelligence.

Tax offices are currently increasing the number and depth of their enquiries into companies' accounts. These enquiries are being carried out by teams rather than by single officers, and to help them, these teams are calling on the skills of the Special Compliance Office (SCO), the Revenue's special forces (see page 39). SCO officers are being used to train and assist teams in their enquiries.

The existence of such 'joint manoeuvres' raises the

disturbing possibility of taxpayers having to attend meetings where there is not only more than one tax inspector present, but where there is also an SCO officer attending as mentor, coach and observer. Traditionally, the presence of an SCO officer has suggested that the Revenue suspect more serious matters are afoot. This may no longer necessarily be the case.

Rules of engagement

There are a number of rules that apply to lesser (non-SCO) engagements with the Revenue:

Number one

The early stages of any skirmish are preoccupied with deadlines. In the first instance, the Revenue have to throw down the gauntlet within a certain period of time. For example, they have to send their initial request for further information, the Mae West letter, within 12 months of the due date of filing – ie, normally by the end of January each year.

So anyone who has not received a letter from the Revenue by January 30th 2004 concerning their tax liability for the year 2001/02 is not going to be subject to a random enquiry. Thereafter, the Revenue can only open an enquiry on the basis of the discovery of material information. Only after 20 years is the taxpayer completely off the hook.

The determination of deadlines is not always as simple as it seems. There have been court cases to determine precisely when deadlines occur. The case of Wing Hung Lai v Bale, for example, established that the relevant date for receiving an enquiry letter from the Revenue is the date when the notice is delivered to the taxpayer, not the date when it was issued by the tax office. Where a notice is sent by second-class post, it is not deemed to have been delivered until the fourth working day after the posting.

War or Peace

Tax inspectors can react very differently to missed deadlines. Some are quite relaxed about them; others follow up immediately and call on their legal rights to impose penalties. The Revenue have issued guidelines on what they consider to be a reasonable excuse for filing a return late, and for paying tax late (see page 21). Not being able to read the fine print of a return is no excuse. The Revenue produce leaflets in Braille, on audio and in large print. Remember that they have heard every excuse in the book – from 'the canary ate it' to 'I had to pay my mother-in-law's hospital bill, so I didn't have any money at the time.'

Major deadlines

January 31st: the deadline for payment of tax due
for the 12-month period to the previous April 5th.

❈❈❈❈

February 28th: penalties imposed for unpaid tax
due on the last day of January (ie, a month ago).

❈❈❈❈

April 6th: tax returns are sent out to all those who
received one a year earlier.

❈❈❈❈

July 31st: extra penalties kick in for late payments
that are still overdue.

❈❈❈❈

September 30th: the date by which returns have to
be received by the Revenue if the taxpayer wants to
be sure that he will receive the Revenue's
estimation of what he owes in time to pay it
without penalty (ie, before January 31st of the
following year). The Revenue will always do the
calculation for you, but if you submit your return
late they will not guarantee to do it before you
move into the penalty zone.

The Revenue will accept as a 'reasonable excuse' for the late filing of a tax return:

☞ Fire or flood at the post office where the tax return was handled.
☞ Prolonged industrial action in the Post Office.
☞ Loss of records through fire, flood or theft (but putting a cigarette lighter to last year's accounts does not work).
☞ Very serious illness, such as coma, major heart attack, stroke or any other serious mental or life-threatening condition (but the possibility of a Revenue enquiry is not itself considered life-threatening).
☞ Death of a close relative or (domestic) partner 'shortly before the deadline' (and don't think that granny's demise ten years ago will count).

The Revenue have also spelt out a number of excuses that they will not accept.

☞ Finding the tax form too difficult to complete.
☞ Pressure of work.
☞ Failure by a tax agent.
☞ Lack of information.
☞ Absence of reminders by the Revenue.
☞ Away on holiday.

In addition, they do not consider 'shortage of funds' to be a reasonable excuse for non-payment of tax.

Remember also, though, that the final decision as to what constitutes a reasonable excuse lies with the tax commissioners (see page 42). The Revenue's guidelines are no more than guidelines. They cannot lay down hard and fast rules. At the end of the day, every case is considered on its merits.

Number two

The Human Rights Act, which came into force in the UK in October 2000, is a sort of Geneva Convention for Revenue skirmishes. It lays down some rules about what can and cannot be done to taxpayers who are taken to task by the Revenue. It does not say anything about having their fingernails removed.

In particular, it introduces a slightly different definition of what constitutes a criminal offence. Any case involving substantial penalties, even one settled under the so-called Hansard Rules (see page 67) may be considered criminal under the Act. One of the consequences of this arises from the fact that criminal liability cannot outlive the criminal. Hence the penalties for the fiscal crimes of the dead may not be visited on their heirs, which goes somewhat against a strict reading of existing UK tax legislation.

The liability to tax and interest is restricted to the six years after death. But the chances of the Revenue arranging an interview with the taxpayer to discuss the finer details are remote, however grave the issue. Sooner or later the inspectors are bound to come to a dead end.

Number three

The Revenue's Code of Practice lays down another rule of engagement: that they 'want you to pay the right amount of tax: no more; no less' and they will do 'everything [they] reasonably can to make sure this happens.' What is the right amount of tax, of course, is in many cases open to discussion. Ten different accountants

---

The Revenue promise that they will:

- Provide clear and simple forms and guidance, and be fair. (The Revenue's forms regularly win prizes for their design and their comprehensible English.)
- Be accessible. They have a help line (0845 9000 444) and can be contacted through their local enquiry centres (the numbers are in the telephone directory).
- Be courteous and professional (like any decent soldier).
- Handle taxpayers' affairs promptly and accurately (ie, they will not extend the torture any longer than is absolutely necessary).

---

working on one individual's tax affairs can come up with ten different amounts payable. And even then the Revenue may come up with an eleventh.

In a recent press release, the Revenue stated that:

Anyone who underestimates profits or income …
should make an early disclosure to the Inland
Revenue. Taxpayers who come forward and make full
disclosure can expect to pay tax, interest and penalties
on the money they have not previously disclosed. But

*if they wait to be prosecuted, they risk not only a
prison sentence, but also confiscation of all monies or
other benefits that they may have made from the crime
of tax evasion.*

Number four

In theory, the Revenue have the right to ask for almost
any information that they fancy. In the first instance, the
taxpayer will be invited to supply the information voluntarily. If it is not provided voluntarily then the Revenue
can use their powers to obtain it in other ways.

In practice, tax officers are told to ask only for information that is relevant, and that can be shown to be
'reasonably' required for the purposes of checking the
taxpayer's return.

The Revenue recently published a ruling on the
subject:

'The overriding test,' they said, 'is based on what is
reasonable (that is, fair and sensible) in the circumstances.' One man's 'sensible', of course, can easily be another man's 'unfair'.

On the contentious issue of private bank accounts,
the Revenue have said: 'The question of whether it is reasonable to request private documents, including bank
and building-society accounts, can only be determined
by reference to the facts in each individual case.' Not
much help there.

The only thing that the Revenue seem prepared to be definite about is that: 'non-business bank details should not be requested in the opening letter as a matter of course.' But even then you can't depend on it. For their guidelines continue: 'However, where accounts are not based on a robust and effectively operated record-keeping system … it would be reasonable to request the private bank details with the other records.' The Revenue have made it clear more recently, however, that in cases concerned only with unverified items of expenditure, it is not appropriate to ask for private bank details. To be safe, though, don't assume that anything is out of bounds – even in the very first opening salvo.

> Complacency is a far more dangerous attitude than outrage.
> *Naomi Littlebear Morena*

There is some comfort to be gleaned from the fact that nowhere does the legislation lay down where the information/documents have to be produced. It is never a good idea to invite the Revenue round to your place to have a look. If you would rather not send the details to them, then try to fight this skirmish on neutral ground – preferably in the offices of your tax adviser. And make sure that some decent refreshments are available (a deductible expense, note) and photocopying facilities. The Revenue have the right (which they are sure to exercise) to take away copies of documents that they consider to be relevant. They have the right to take the original copies too, but a taxpayer can demand those back at any time.

If the information is on a computer file of some sort, then offer the Revenue a print-out. These days they have some computer software that can aggressively interrogate

Cornered?

(The questionnaire given to taxpayers who have been caught)

1 Have any transactions been omitted from or incorrectly recorded in the books of any business with which you are or have been concerned, whether as a director, partner or sole proprietor?

2 Are the accounts sent to the Inland Revenue for any business with which you are or have been concerned as a director, partner or sole proprietor correct and complete to the best of your knowledge and belief?

3 Are all of the tax returns of any business with which you are or have been concerned whether as a director, partner or sole proprietor correct and complete to the best of your knowledge?

4 Are all your personal tax returns correct and complete to the best of your knowledge and belief?

If you can honestly answer 'no' to the first question and 'yes' to each of the others, you have nothing to worry about.

electronic accounting packages. So it's better that they don't get hold of them in the first place.

The Revenue and HM Customs & Excise have swapped information legally for some time. But information disclosed by taxpayers to the Revenue went no further than that. Or at least it didn't until the Anti-Terrorism Act of 2001, which followed the attacks of September 11th that year. That legislation gave the Revenue permission to disclose information to others for purposes of national security and for criminal investigations.

Combined with an increased determination to crack down on money laundering through greater sharing of information, it has knocked a huge hole in the wall of confidentiality that used to encircle the Revenue and their affairs. For instance, it permits information about taxpayers to be disclosed for the purposes of any criminal investigation whatsoever which is being (or may be) carried out anywhere, either in the UK or elsewhere. The traditional assumption that other government departments in the UK (and most tax authorities abroad) were going to be neither interested in, nor have access to information provided to the Revenue is no longer valid.

Apart from this gaping hole, officials may not disclose information about an identifiable taxpayer (that has not already been made lawfully available to the public) other than with the lawful consent of the taxpayer. In its own literature, the Revenue say that they will 'treat your affairs in strict confidence, within the law.'

The Revenue are also subject to other legislation which protects the privacy of the individual – the Data Protection Act, for example, and the Convention on Human Rights (see page 22).

The Data Protection Act gives data providers (and that means you) the right to be told what information is held on them by bodies such as the Revenue. In most cases this is not a problem for tax inspectors. The Revenue are only too happy (for the fee that the law demands be paid) to provide taxpayers with copies of their returns and the supporting documents that they hold. In February 2002, the Revenue said that they 'aim to respond to requests for information under the act within the 40-day time limit … [and] have in place a small central unit whose role is to co-ordinate, manage and oversee the responses to all requests for information under the Data Protection Act.'

There is a difficulty, however, in cases where the Revenue are carrying out an investigation. Inspectors often begin by indicating to taxpayers that they hold certain information which suggests that the taxpayer's return is less than perfect – in the hope of persuading the taxpayer to fill in the gaps. If the Revenue were legally required to reveal what that information was, at the request of the taxpayer, it would considerably weaken one of their major strategic weapons. This is still a grey area yet to be tested in the courts.

Number five

A taxpayer has the right to complain about the Revenue, and the number of complaints being lodged is increasing sharply. Complaints range from the 'bullying' tactics of inspectors to long delays in carrying out investigations.

The legislation which empowers the Revenue to carry out enquiries into self-assessment returns contains no specific right of appeal against the enquiry itself. The balance of power is shifted somewhat by the right given to taxpayers to ask the tax commissioners (see page 42) to instruct the inspector to bring an enquiry to an end within a specified amount of time. In theory, a taxpayer could make such a request as soon as he received notice of the Revenue's enquiry. In practice, he would be unlikely to receive a favourable ruling until the inspector had had time to collect and consider the information requested from the taxpayer.

If a taxpayer receives a letter requesting an actual meeting with his tax inspector, it is fair to assume that the Revenue think they have reasonable grounds to doubt the accuracy of the taxpayer's return. But the taxpayer is under absolutely no obligation to attend such a meeting. In fact, he is usually well advised to stay away and let his adviser handle the matter. Long experience shows that taxpayers tend to convey the wrong message on such occasions.

In one case, a taxpayer emerged from a meeting with the Revenue in London's High Holborn. As soon as he got onto the street he started jumping up and down with glee. What he hadn't realised was that the inspector was watching him from an upper window. He went straight from High Holborn into Deep Water.

War or Peace

The combatants

There are several groups of participants in most battles with the Revenue. First and foremost, there is the taxman himself.

The tax inspectors

Inspectors work out of a number of different offices. So-called 'local offices' (they're not necessarily local to the taxpayer) deal with the vast majority of tax affairs. But there are also 'special offices', which deal with industry-wide problems. The entertainment industry, for instance, has a special office based in Gateshead.

Then there are things called LBOs (Large Business Offices) which deal with complicated cases of transfer pricing – where companies try to shift profits to low-tax jurisdictions by artificially inflating the costs of intra-group transfers. And there are what are known as Large Business Offices (Employer Compliance). These deal with the affairs of employees at companies with more

than 1,000 people on their payroll. Finally, there is the SCO, the Special Compliance Office (see page 39).

Tax inspectors are invariably curious. They're interested in people (it's a qualification for the job) and they like to go out on recces. They keep an eye out for expensive alterations to houses in their neighbourhood, for example, and they read the local newspapers. Nowadays they also like to surf the net.

They soon pick up investigative skills, or they change their career. One inspector, for example, calling

on a small private company, decided to take a quick snoop round the car park before he entered the company's offices. There he noticed a particularly smart Jaguar.

Later, when the meeting with the company's managing director was in full swing, the inspector raised the question of the director's mileage claim on his P11D, the form that records an employee's expenses. The director went into raptures about his Jaguar and said that it was a pleasure to use it on business. 'Yes,' said the inspector, 'I see you claim to do about 18,000 miles a year in it.' 'That's right,' said the managing director. 'Can't get enough of it.' 'Then how come,' said the inspector drily, 'that there's only 9,000 miles on the clock?'

The Revenue are also skilled at using the government's forensic laboratories. Their capability enables them to analyse the age of inks. Faking invoices or receipts for years gone by can soon be exposed. And don't claim that you filled in the Revenue's forms before you did. They all have a code which reveals exactly when they were printed.

> Remember the wartime slogan: 'Careless talk costs lives'. It can cost a whole load of extra tax too.

Furthermore, never underestimate a tax inspector's grasp of trivia. A recent query on an accounting web site asked what to do about a client who claimed that a particular type of tray could carry more than six ounces of rice whilst his inspector alleged that it could take only three ounces. The query provided rich food for thought, sparking off a range of replies from 'Paddy Fields', 'Uncle Ben', 'Roger Rabbit' and others. One respondent alleged that the Revenue have a special unit dedicated to answering such questions. Other issues that the unit has tackled recently include, apparently, the vexing question of 'How many £5 notes can fit in a shoebox?'

In their literature, the Revenue say that inspectors like to meet taxpayers face-to-face. Many of them at the local level, however, are not trained to handle full-frontal confrontations with aggressive entrepreneurs. For the most part, they would prefer to carry out their skirmishing by post. There are exceptions, however. At a face-to-face meeting with one inspector, a company accountant was so taken aback by the inspector's aggressive introductory statement that he was 'on a crusade against troncs' (the way waiters' tips are recorded) that the

> ### The Revenue have set out the cases where they might be tempted to put the SCO's sleuths into action:
>
> - Where there has been creativity involved (falsification of documents, for example, or backdating).
> - Where a professional adviser is suspected of dishonesty.
> - Where a certificate of disclosure signed by a taxpayer turns out to be false.
> - Where there is suspected fraud using offshore vehicles.

accountant showed him all sorts of company books that he was under no obligation to reveal.

The Revenue have recently agreed to produce an agenda covering the main points for discussion before any meeting takes place. This is a reversal of previous policy, when they refused to limit the scope for discussion by producing an agenda in advance. After every such meeting, the Revenue produce a written record, and the taxpayer has the right to ask for (and receive!) a copy.

The tax inspector's aim in meetings will normally be to make the taxpayer feel as relaxed as possible before getting him to talk in an unguarded way about his affairs. A classic question marks the switch from the warm-up to the battle proper. This is: 'Now tell me about your business.' Watch out for it. Forewarned is forearmed.

A basic assumption in most detective stories is that if you give a guilty man enough rope he will hang himself. Encourage him to talk long enough and he will incriminate himself. Tax inspectors work on the same principle.

Inspectors are not always efficient – and neither are their computer systems. In one widely publicised incident, they admitted to losing over a million taxpayers' records for 1997–98 without being sure whether the taxpayers in question had paid the correct amounts. In a more recent confession, the Revenue admitted that they were still dealing with post that they had received four months earlier.

The Special Compliance Office

Officers who work in the Special Compliance Office (SCO) of the Revenue are the taxman's elite squad. They are only brought out for the more serious battles, those where the amounts and offences involved are expected to be significant. The SCO, for example, is unlikely to follow a case involving less than £100,000 of unpaid tax.

The rights and tactics of the SCO are very different from those of local inspectors. Another BDO Stoy Hayward publication, *An Inspector Returns* (Profile Books, 2002), describes what an unsettling experience an SCO investigation can be. Many of the headline cases that hit

In *An Inspector Returns* we laid out ten golden rules to be followed by a taxpayer who comes under investigation by the SCO:

1 Keep calm and don't panic.

2 Get expert advice. It's always the cheaper option.

3 Don't discuss your tax affairs with anyone but a tight circle of professional advisers.

4 Don't lie to the Revenue.

5 Don't assume that the Revenue are ignorant of anything.

6 Be well prepared for meetings. People don't plan to fail; they fail to plan.

7 Make significant (but relevant) payments on account. According to the Revenue, there is no better sign of co-operation with them.

8 Don't try to destroy evidence. It's usually unhelpful.

9 Don't suffer from selective amnesia when disclosing information involuntarily.

10 Once you've reached a settlement, don't offend again. The Revenue don't look kindly on serial evaders.

With minor modifications, these rules apply to any Revenue investigation.

the newspapers are, in fact, investigations by the SCO. An entrepreneur whose farmhouse and offices were searched by as many as ten inspectors in a dawn raid recently received widespread press coverage. The raid was carried out by the SCO, and a number of computers and documents were removed. Such an investigation is unusual, however, and requires the tax officers to obtain a search warrant from a judge.

Like all crack military units, the SCO is used on occasions to boost run-of-the-mill footsoldiers. At the same time, the SCO itself is being boosted by the recruitment of a number of forensic accountants whose job it is to dig into dubious company accounts.

The tax commissioners

If a taxpayer wants to appeal against a decision of the Revenue, his first recourse is to the tax commissioners. These are independent tribunals which sit in judgement on disputed issues.

There are two kinds of commissioner. General commissioners consider general matters – such as whether a taxpayer's excuse for paying his tax late is 'reasonable'. The second kind, special commissioners, are bodies of tax experts who hear cases which involve interpretation of the law. Recent cases heard by special commissioners involved:

- A dispute over transfer pricing (the recorded costs of activities carried out between individual companies within the same group).
- Whether a taxpayer could subsequently claim that there was a mistake in a return for a year which he had already agreed with the Revenue to be closed.

The general commissioners tend to be businessmen; the special commissioners tend to be accountants or lawyers.

The general commissioners have three main roles:

- They rule on contentious issues, such as appeals by a taxpayer against a Revenue assessment.
- They decide whether a taxpayer has a 'reasonable' excuse for being late in filing a return or supplying information requested by the Revenue.
- They can instruct the Revenue to amend penalties or to close down an enquiry.

Special commissions are a bit like a court and can be intimidating. General commissions, by contrast, are much more relaxed and informal, held usually sitting round a table. It is often a good idea for taxpayers to attend these hearings. The general commissioners are quite likely to be on their side. If a taxpayer is claiming, for instance, that he has been ill, and he really looks ill, the chances are it will move the commissioners in his favour.

Both the taxpayer and the Revenue have the right to appeal directly to the courts against a judgement of the commissioners. But such a move is sure to prove costly. There is, however, no right of appeal on a matter of fact. When the commissioners decide the facts, their version becomes the ultimate truth.

> The definition of 'ultimate truth' is 'what the inspector accepts' or 'what the commissioners decide'.

There have been far fewer referrals to the commissioners since self-assessment began. Before it, the commissioners were often asked to rule on whether an assessment had been properly raised by the Revenue. Now that the onus is on the taxpayer to raise the assessment, such cases no longer arise.

One of the prime remaining responsibilities of the general commissioners (given to them by parliament) is to decide what is a reasonable excuse (see page 21) – either for sending in a return late or for paying tax late. Commissioners do not take kindly to being told by the Revenue what their decision in such cases should be. They are also the ultimate arbiter in fixing the level of penalties.

The taxpayers

Taxpayers come in all shapes and sizes. Some of them are petrified by the prospect of any sort of tussle with the Revenue; others become unbelievably belligerent and aggressive before any sort of wrongdoing has been established. There will always be a few people who are prepared to argue with a lamp-post if no more stimulating option is available.

Note that the Revenue like taxpayers to use their proper names in all their tax affairs. Inspectors were not amused by the restaurant chain that recorded one of its employees as 'Chicken Tikka Masala', or another restaurant that had 'Frog One', 'Frog Two' and 'Frog Three' on its payroll.

Tax inspectors take no view of the morality of taxpayers. Their sole interest is in collecting tax that is due. The Revenue can tax illegal activities. The proceeds from crime are not taxable but profits from a trade carried on illegally are. Americans are taxed on their income regardless of whether it has been legitimately earned or not. Hence when drug dealers are identified and imprisoned in the US, they are likely to receive a demand from the IRS, America's Internal Revenue Service. In the UK, when smoking cannabis is legalised, inspectors will no doubt be on the streets sniffing out the trade and seeking their share of it. They are renowned for following their noses – all in the course of duty.

> Life has no romance without risk.

Prostitution can be legal under certain circumstances in the UK. In such a cash-oriented business, however, collecting what is due to the Revenue is not always easy.

In one instance, however, they struck gold by ringing the number in an advertisement placed in *Time Out* magazine. The lady turned out to be a very high-earner indeed. Her clients included a number of well-known figures prepared to pay several thousand pounds a time for her services, both by credit card and/or cash.

When the Revenue began to dig into her income they could only attempt to calculate it by going over her expenses and looking at her assets – which included several high-powered cars and a number of luxury homes. In the end, they were forced to make her bankrupt and seize her property in order to collect some of the tax that was due on her substantial income.

Family-owned companies are often easy pickings for the Revenue because so many of their proprietors consider the company to be theirs for the plundering. Some try to pass every possible thing through the family business as an expense. But not all of them are very subtle about it. One company owner tried to pass his mother's Sainsbury's receipts through the books, most of them dated on a Saturday and many of them including such essential business accoutrements as 'nappies' and 'tights'.

The man would not even stop at his own family's expenses. He produced two receipts from one garage issued on the same day within half an hour of each other. One was for petrol and the other for diesel. While filling his own car he had picked up someone else's discarded receipt. The Revenue suspected that he had also been col-

lecting receipts from the floor around supermarket tills –
extraordinary how low some taxpayers will stoop.

> The best armour is to keep out of range.
> *Italian proverb*

People who join with others to work together as a
partnership are treated differently by the Revenue in at
least one important respect. Not only does each partner
(and there can be anything between two and a few hun-
dred of them) have to send in his own individual tax
return, but the partnership itself has to submit a return as
well, signed by a nominated partner.

The Revenue can raise an enquiry into this partnership return just as they can raise an enquiry into the returns
of any of the individual partners. The effects of this can
sometimes be awkward. If anything changes in the partnership return, the consequences can ripple out to all the
partners individually and compel each of them to change
their personal returns. For example, suppose the Revenue
had agreed to a general rule that 75 per cent of the cost of
the partners' cars was an allowable business expense. But
they then changed their mind and said that henceforth
only 50 per cent would be allowed. Every partner who
used their car for business purposes would be affected.

Insiders

Recent legislation makes it clear that it is not just an offence for a taxpayer to cheat, but it is also an offence for someone to help a taxpayer to cheat. 'A person commits an offence if he is knowingly concerned in the fraudulent evasion of income tax by him or any other person.'

This has been designed specifically to catch cases where employers and employees collude to pay the latter in cash (outside the PAYE and national insurance systems) knowing that it will enable the 'employee' to continue to claim benefits. Typical cases involve casual workers on building sites, the sort that are picked up at

And that's Malone — He investigates the building site scams

road junctions in major cities by little white vans very early in the morning.

The use of the phrase 'fraudulent evasion' in this context has led to some comment. There was always an understanding that 'tax avoidance' was the legal practice – nay, the right of every individual to avoid paying more tax than the absolute minimum required by law. Tax evasion, on the other hand, was the illegal avoidance of tax. Now we have 'fraudulent evasion', suggesting that there is a kind of evasion which is not fraudulent – ie, not done with dishonest intent ... but dishonest none the less. Confusing, isn't it?

Informers

The tax authorities rely heavily on informers and, luckily for them, human beings have an amazing capacity to grass on each other. Since 1890 the Revenue have been entitled to give informers a reward for their efforts. But most people are quite happy to blab for nothing.

The Revenue have a special 'Criminal Investigation Hotline' (0800 829 0433) for informers to use. Callers are not required to identify themselves, although they will be encouraged to do so, on the understanding that their identity will be kept confidential.

Taxpayers often have families, and when they start to feel the pressure of an engagement with the Revenue they like to talk about their worries with their

nearest and dearest. The trouble with today's families, though, is that they don't last as long as they used to. Last year's nearest and dearest can be this year's jilted lover. And the Revenue have no source of revealing information more fruitful than the jilted lover. Every tax inspector knows that hell hath no fury like a woman scorned.

Jilted lovers often have the attitude that if their former partner is going to live without them, then that part-

ner is also going to live without lots of other things besides. These include things like the undeclared offshore income that may in the past have enabled the informer to spend frequent holidays in Marbella and Monte Carlo, dressed in a style to which she has since had to become unaccustomed.

Former spouses can also be a problem. Things that have been hidden from the taxman during a marriage can suddenly be flushed out into the open when the partners are seeking a divorce settlement. In one case, a sales rep for a book publisher was in court for his divorce hearing. His wife explained how each rep was given two copies of every book that the firm published (about 1,000 books at an average retail price, then, of £5). Reps generally keep the books they want – a small proportion – and then sell off the rest at a discount to book shops. It is a well-known perk of the trade. Unfortunately for this rep – and every other rep in the sales force – a tax inspector was waiting in the court for the judge to hear his own divorce. It took the publishing firm four years to sort out and pay the huge back-payments of tax for its reps.

In another case, a husband had claimed to the Revenue that the house where he and his wife lived was owned by an offshore company. When the divorce came to be discussed in court, the wife managed to prove that the house belonged to the husband, and that half of it was hers. The Revenue were particularly interested to read the divorce judge's statement that 'by virtue of some transaction not explained, or not properly explained, the husband was able to assemble offshore monies which later he deployed in the purchase'. Such judgements are confidential. But the wife's brother felt that this particular one should be brought to the attention of the Revenue.

If the driving force is not sex gone sour, then it's probably money gone sour. In one scam run by a company which had three garages carrying out quick repairs, one of the two people who were not benefiting from the scam decided to blow the whistle.

All the cash jobs at these garages went into a kitty which was shared around on Fridays. Everybody who worked there benefited except the receptionist and the (rather selfless) managing director. Needless to say, the receptionist called the Revenue one day, and inspectors arranged to raid the premises at a time when she was for-tuitously not at work.

The only people who got prosecuted were the garage's managing director and the man who signed the company's P35 forms – a part-time accountant who was fined £5 for every form he had signed incorrectly over the seven-year period that the scam had been under way. The total amount of the fine was £35,000. In addition, the accountant received a suspended prison sentence.

The advisers

When the taxman comes calling, your first thought may be: 'Help, I need help'. And indeed, you probably do. But many people hesitate to seek advice. Most tax advisers are accountants first and foremost, and accountants have traditionally been held in low esteem – typically known as people who solve problems you didn't know you had in a way you don't understand.

As far as the Revenue are concerned you can choose to be professionally represented at any stage in the pro-ceedings, and you can change adviser at any stage. The Revenue will deal with whoever you tell them to. If you use a reputable and experienced adviser/guide, the benefits almost always outweigh the disadvantages. The guide who can tell you which part of the forest to avoid when you are trying to skirt round the enemy is worth more than his weight in machine guns.

One big advantage of having an agent is the ongoing communication that has been established between the agent and the Revenue. An agent, for example, will phone the Revenue if a deadline is approaching and fend off the risk of a heavy-handed reminder. It's a rare taxpayer who will feel sufficiently

relaxed about his tax affairs to ring an inspector and tell him that he's going to be late sending in the forms that have been requested.

Other advantages of using an agent:

- If you have expenditure, and it is debatable whether it is deductible or not, evidence that a reputable firm has looked at it and made a judgement about it does help in persuading the Revenue of your case.
- Professional advisers are dealing with tax inspectors every day of their lives. If they don't understand them, nobody does.

An inspector from Liverpool was in a tight skirmish with a taxpayer, his only ally being the most potent weapon known to man – the truth. The taxpayer was cornered, awaiting his fate (almost certain bankruptcy) when out comes his adviser waving a current 'Official Liverpool Supporters' Club' membership card. The result? The Revenue immediately called a truce, eventually surrendered and finally, in extra time, paid a refund – with interest too.

Some balk at using an adviser because of the cost. But most long-serving advisers believe that if they had been working on a contingency basis – earning a percentage of the tax that they legitimately save their clients – they would today be very rich indeed.

Taxpayers who want to guard against the cost of buying such advice can sometimes take out insurance to cover any professional fees that might be involved in an Inland Revenue investigation. But they should take a close look at the small print of any such policy. In many cases that we have seen it renders them virtually useless.

There is a chance, of course, that if you are caught skirting the enemy in the company of a known dodgy guide, it will not reflect well on you. The Revenue used to have a black book which contained the names of known dodgy agents. Anyone whose returns were filled in by these agents was likely to get a 'random' enquiry. At the local level, such blacklists are probably still kept today.

Advisers are, however, being put under increasing pressure to behave properly. Not only are they far more likely than an ordinary taxpayer to end up in prison should they commit a criminal offence, but they are also expected to have a full knowledge of the law. Ignorance, never a very good excuse, is a useless plea for an adviser. As Lord Denning once said: in law, 'ignorance is a misfortune, not a privilege'.

In one recent case, the Court of Appeal said, 'when professional advisers are found to have acted dishonestly towards the Revenue, it is almost inevitable ... that sentences of prison must follow.'

At the end of the day, though, everyone is responsible for their own returns. Agents cannot be held responsible for things that their clients have never told them.

> ### What is the difference between a prisoner and a PAYE employee?
>
> *A prisoner has all his expenses paid by the taxpayer without being required to work. A PAYE employee pays all his own expenses in order to go to work. And then he has taxes deducted from his salary in order to pay for the prisoners.*

Prisoners of war

Finally, there are those combatants who get caught. Not many of them actually end up in prison. The majority reach an agreement with the Revenue, pay their unpaid tax plus some fines and penalties (see page 100), and then go off and earn some more money ... to be declared on their next return. They are freed to fight again, to earn

> Another difference between prisoners
> and PAYE employees:
>
> *Prisoners spend much of their life inside bars
> wanting to get out.*
> *PAYE employees spend much of their life wanting to get
> out so that they can get inside bars.*

more taxable income. And there's nothing the Revenue like more than that.

The strategies

There are a number of simple strategic steps that taxpayers can take to increase the odds against being subjected to an enquiry – to keep their heads below the parapet, as it were, and to avoid coming into the direct line of fire. One of them is to make sure that they provide the Revenue with enough information to avoid arousing their suspicions in the first place.

Allied to that is the need to keep adequate records so that the Revenue's questions (if and when they come) can be answered easily. The Revenue suggest that taxpayers 'should keep everything you need to fill in your tax return or to make a claim. This includes all documents (whether paper or electronic) that you used to reach each figure.'

When the self-assessment procedure first started (in 1996/97), there was a feeling that it was best to give the inspectors a minimum amount of information, and to leave it up to them to ask for anything extra that they might need. Nowadays, however, that view has changed,

Ways of reducing the chance of an enquiry

Popular view:

- Don't keep records: follow the Enron principle – debit, credit and then shred it.
- Only use cash.
- Keep nothing in the UK.
- Don't sell anything to anybody.
- Don't tell anything to anybody.
- Live on Mars.

Reality:

- Make sure your tax returns are filed on time.
- Pay any tax due on time.
- Don't be greedy.
- Don't tell lies.

largely because inspectors who find they are short of one particular bit of information are tempted to look and see what else might be missing.

In one case, for instance, a taxpayer had a valuation of a property done for tax purposes by his brother. His brother was a professional chartered surveyor and there was no suggestion that the valuation was anything other than fair and independent. It was decided, however, not to mention to the Revenue who had done the valuation. When the Revenue noticed the omission and asked the taxpayer for the name of the valuer, of course it all began to look pear shaped. Suspicions were unjustifiably aroused.

Honesty really is the best policy. And be honest right from the beginning. It is not a good idea to get there gradually. In one case, the proprietor of a successful small engineering firm stashed away for years the cash proceeds of a scrap metal business that he was running on the side. When caught by the Revenue, he at first confessed that the proceeds had been used to buy a bungalow in a well-known south-coast resort. When pressed as to whether that was the sum total of it, he admitted that, actually, he also owned the bungalow next door. By the time the Revenue had finished with him, it had emerged that he owned almost a whole street of bungalows. He was lucky not to be prosecuted and to end up in prison. As it was, the penalties exacted by the Revenue were, understandably, heavy.

Tactics in the field

Tactics are the day-to-day measures taken in the field in order to fulfil a combatant's overall strategy. An important tactic in battles with the Revenue is, don't try to be funny. Tax inspectors do have a sense of humour, but it is not always predictable. The taxpayer who put 'F. All' in the box asking for 'other income' was lucky. At first the inspector wrote to say that this sort of comment was not appropriate in what was, after all, a legal document. But he withdrew his objection when informed by the taxpayer that he had intended 'F. All' to stand for 'Family Allowance'.

The inspectors were also not very amused by the director of a family business who insisted that a journey with his girlfriend to Amsterdam either side of Valentine's Day was a genuine business trip.

Attitude counts in dealings with the Revenue. In one case, an inspector had evidence that some fees paid by a hospital to a doctor who was employed by a practice

It is not a good idea to lose your temper with the taxman. The managing director mentioned earlier (whose fraudulent claim for travelling expenses in his Jaguar was exposed by a canny inspector) threw a fit when his scam was revealed. He walked around screaming and shouting and threatening to get the milometer 'fixed' to prove his claim. He was so insulting that the inspector left immediately and initiated a full inspection of the company's accounts. If the man had been reasonably polite, the inspector would probably not have dug any further.

were not being declared. The inspector chose to insti-
gate a full-blown enquiry (even though the tax involved
was very small) because he felt the taxpayer's attitude to
things like expenses was far too casual. 'Let's say
they're about the same as last year,' is not the sort of
reply that the Revenue like to hear.

Taxpayers who protest their innocence the loudest
are usually those with something to hide. They happen
to be skilled enough at self-delusion to have convinced
themselves that they really are not cheating the taxman.
But, believe it or not, tax inspectors read Shakespeare.
'Methinks he doth protest too much,' is one of their
favourite quotes from the bard.

It helps if taxpayers volunteer early on to make a payment on account when the Revenue are establishing that there is a hitherto undisclosed tax liability. According to the Revenue, there is no better sign that the tax-payer is co-operating with them. And co-operation is an important element in the circumstances leading to the mitigation of penalties (see page 103).

Bargaining with the Revenue is always possible. In many cases, the precise tax liability is a matter of judgement and interpretation. Rather than pursue the case in the courts, the Revenue will often prefer to come to an agreement that enables them then to close the case with honour.

In cases of tax fraud, the Revenue have been given exceptional bargaining powers, known as the Hansard Rules (after the name of the official published report of Britain's parliamentary proceedings – see box opposite).

When a taxpayer is interrogated under the Hansard Rules, he is tempted to give away things which, under a more normal criminal investigation, he would be advised not to mention. The Revenue cannot take advantage of his confession.

Sometimes, of course, the Revenue make tactical errors, just as taxpayers and their advisers do. In one case, a self-employed man had a sophisticated accounting package on his laptop which he used in making his tax returns. The Revenue opened an enquiry into the week-end visits to CenterParcs that the man was claiming as an expense. But the inspector completely failed to pick up

The Hansard Rules

In November 2002, Hansard published a revised response from the Chancellor of the Exchequer to a parliamentary question. In his reply, the Chancellor confirmed and updated the rules on bargaining, which have come to be known as the Hansard Rules:

1. The Revenue may accept a money settlement instead of pursuing criminal proceedings in cases where fraud is alleged to have been committed by a taxpayer.
2. The Revenue will accept a money settlement and will not pursue a criminal prosecution if the taxpayer makes a full and complete confession of all tax irregularities.

There are plenty of people eager to advise taxpayers of ways in which they can reduce the amount of tax that they pay. Some of the ways that such people recommend are perfectly legal; some are not. America's Internal Revenue Service warns taxpayers not to fall victim to tax scams, and it lists eight scams that are particularly common. 'Taxpayers need to remember,' it says, 'that if it sounds too good to be true, it probably is.'

> The Revenue once sent out a request for information to:
>
> *Mr F. Smith (deceased)*
> *Croydon Crematorium.*
>
> When the letter was eventually forwarded to Mr Smith's widow she (not surprisingly) lodged an official complaint.

the fact that the man was invoicing and being paid regularly (and almost exclusively) by a single source. He should not have been self-employed at all; he should have been subject to PAYE.

There are more general cases where tax law designed to catch a particular type of avoidance (or to encourage a specific type of behaviour) catches or encourages a completely different type of behaviour. Take the case of the 'two years rule', introduced by the Revenue to encourage employees to be more mobile within the UK. The incentive payment made to encourage a worker to move from, say, Bristol, to a temporary post in Scunthorpe is tax-free. But the Revenue failed to appreciate that such a rule could also embrace expatriates moving to the UK on 'temporary secondment'. Workers coming from, say, South Africa on secondment to the UK can now enjoy many expenses whilst in the UK tax-free. This has been known to be as much as £2,000 a month.

The causes of war

Status

There are a number of classic issues over which skirmishes are fought again and again between taxpayers and the Revenue. One of the most notable is the fight to establish whether an individual employee should be put on a company's PAYE (Pay As You Earn) system or be self-employed. Most people would prefer to be self-employed: it means that they pay tax later (PAYE is deducted at source), and it makes them believe that they can deduct more generous expenses from their pre-tax earnings.

The issue of a taxpayer's status (PAYE or self-employed) is a difficult one and not always clear cut. The issue can, however, be resolved right from the beginning. The employer or the employee (and, under the self-assessment system, it is primarily the employee's responsibility to make sure that he or she is correctly classified) can get a ruling in advance from the Revenue as to whether they should be PAYE or self-employed (and so be assessed under what is called 'Schedule D'). Many people, however, prefer to leave the issue vague in the hope that after the event they will receive the more favourable ruling. If that means that tax, which ultimately has to be paid, is in the meanwhile dissipated on old wine and new clothes, it is probably not a good idea.

It is surprising how often businesses have two people doing exactly the same job, yet allow one to be self-employed and the other to be on the payroll. At one famous London restaurant, the summertime cloakroom girls were on PAYE, but the girls who did the same job in winter were self-employed. The winter birds argued that they were just passing through on a round-the-world trip from Australia. Not surprisingly, the Revenue said that their migratory status was irrelevant to their tax status. It was the same job, winter or summer, and therefore the job had to be treated in the same way, regardless of who was doing it.

In certain industries the status issue is particularly difficult. Construction, for example – an industry that now has special legislation to deal with the temporary nature of much of its workforce.

Entertainment is another difficult area. In the film industry, virtually everybody is self-employed. It is rare to find full-time employees in that business. Even the biggest Holywood stars spend long periods 'resting' between engagements. However, a taxpayer's status goes with the work that they are doing, not with the work that they wish they were doing. Two women working as receptionists for an advertising agency were both resting actresses. As actresses they were assessed under Schedule D. But the work that they were doing – being receptionists – was not self-employed. And the employer was compelled to put them on the payroll.

The Revenue have a special unit in Gateshead which deals only with the TV and film industry. And they have another, called the Foreign Entertainers Unit (the FEU), to handle cases where highly-paid foreign entertainers come to the UK to carry out brief engagements for which they are paid large sums of money. When American stars come over for brief appearances in a London theatre, tax should be withheld at source from their (relatively) modest fee. Under the double-taxation agreement between the UK and the United States, the taxpayer is then able to offset tax withheld at source in the UK against any liability that he or she may have to American tax on the same income.

Journalists are another profession whose 'status' is particularly hard to define. Those who work essentially as freelance writers, but who provide material on a regular basis for a particular publication, are now expected to be assessed under PAYE – even if they only contribute every third Friday of the month. There was a time when the mere fact of their being 'freelance' was enough to ensure that they qualified for Schedule D status.

Nowadays, the Revenue are trying to get as many

people off Schedule D as possible – ironically, at the same time as more and more people want to be on it. Taxpayers who switch from being PAYE to being self-employed have three months in which to inform the Revenue of their change of status.

In general, the distinction revolves around the regularity with which people are paid. If they receive cheques from the same source at more or less the same time of the month, then they should be included on that source's payroll.

Sometimes the need to be included on a business's payroll can creep up on a taxpayer almost unawares. Consultants, for example, may genuinely start out doing a one-off job for a client, which soon becomes a two- or three-off job. Before they know where they are, the job has become something that the consultant is being asked to do in the second week of every other month. At which stage, in theory, the taxpayer has to ensure that he is listed on the client's payroll. In practice, it is usually three months or more before they do actually sign up – a somewhat inefficient method of conscription.

Benefits

Another issue which causes many a skirmish between taxpayers and the Revenue is the question of what is a taxable benefit and what is not. This is an area tinged with many shades of grey.

Start with entertainment

It is a basic principle with the Revenue that nobody actually goes to Henley, Twickenham, Wimbledon or Ascot for business. The 'benefit' of attending these occasions at somebody else's expense is taxable. The Revenue are interested in these events for several reasons. Inspectors have been seen scouring the streets of Henley, Wimbledon and Ascot as the great events there are taking place. But the only winners they are interested in are the local residents who have rented out their houses for the occasion, and who may be tempted to forget the large cash sums that they receive for their sacrifice.

All company jaunts are deemed dubious. Unless you work for a truly multinational organisation with offices and operations all around the globe, the Revenue find it hard to believe that an employer can justify holding company gatherings in places like Mauritius or Martinique. Not only can the company not claim all of that as a genuine business expense, but the employees who go on the jaunt may find that the benefit derived from it is being added to their P11D.

But the taxman is no Scrooge. Christmas parties are another matter, and there is a specific Revenue ruling about them. It is a bit like the ceasefires negotiated between British and German troops in the trenches of the first world war. On Christmas Day, soldiers of the two sides shared Christmas fare and played football

Going out to lunch with someone is not always a great pleasure for company accountants. For there is a very thin line between what is allowable and what is not.

Suppose that two employees, Ted and Bill, go out to discuss together a business meeting that they are to have with a customer, Fred. If they claim the meal from their employer it becomes a taxable benefit that has to be included on their P11D form at the end of the year. Likewise, if Ted takes his secretary out for lunch as a reward for having done a particularly hard week's work, and then claims it back from his employer, that is a benefit to both of them. It should be declared on the P11D not only of Ted, but also of his secretary.

A benefit may well be judged to have arisen in the following situations as well:

- When sandwiches are provided on the premises at a board meeting where only directors are present.
- Where the cost of a meal taken on the way home after a late night at the office is reimbursed.

If Ted, Bill and Fred were to go out to lunch together to discuss a contract that they were about to sign, and they were then to claim the cost of the lunch from their company, that would not be a benefit to any of them. Ah well. Nobody said it would be straightforward.

among themselves. By Boxing Day they were sniping at each other again.

Generally, a company's Christmas parties are tax-free as long as they are open to all staff and do not cost more than £75 a head. Also tax-free are the subsidised meals provided to employees on the employer's business premises, so long as the meals are reasonable (ie, no caviar or champagne) and available to all.

For the poor harassed corporate footsoldier, sent out to find new sales outlets, there is a special concession for their newspapers, mini-bars and videos. These so-called 'personal incidental expenses' are tax-free up to £5 a night in the UK and up to £10 a night overseas – not an amount, incidentally, that will cover the cost of an evening's viewing of a Pay-TV pornographic channel in a hotel room in Hanover.

Transport

The rules on the use of cars for company purposes have been simplified in recent years. There was a time when a company car was just about the most generous perk an employee could hope for, but not any more. Much of that benefit is now taxable.

Nevertheless, taxpayers do still manage to have some amazing near-misses on the roads. In a recent case, a taxpayer trading as Fagomatic supplied and serviced cigarette machines to London clubs. To carry out his business, the company's owner bought himself a Lamborghini Diablo car and claimed back the £19,571 of VAT paid on the car, arguing that he had bought it for the sole purpose of gaining competitive advantage. By impressing his customers, he argued, he would be able to stay ahead of the competition. He also claimed that it had never been his intention to use the car privately, and that he had never in fact done so. He worked such long hours, he said, that he had no time for a private life!

The VAT tribunal to which his case was referred accepted both these points. But on appeal to the courts the tribunal's decision was overturned. The court said that 'the very fact of his deliberate acquisition of the car, whereby he makes himself the owner of the car and controller of it, means that at least ordinarily he must intend to make it available to himself for private use, even if he never intends to use it privately.' Quite a fine point that one. Had Fagomatic won its case, however, the implications would have been widespread and dramatic – not least for the market in Lamborghini Diablos.

One commentator described Fagomatic's victory in the tribunal as a bit like an FA Cup tie in which Carlisle is 1–0 ahead against Manchester United at half-time, only to lose 2–1 at the end of the game.

The Revenue's policy on company cars is now environmentally friendly: the amount that is taxable is determined according to the CO_2 emission value of the

It is easy to be tripped up over travel claims – particularly when they concern journeys abroad. The Revenue will ask questions, for example, if on your regular business trips to Hong Kong you always call in at Geneva on the way back. You can tell them that your granny lives there and you like to visit her. But they might ask you to explain why you always visit her on the way back from Hong Kong, and not on the way there.

vehicle. The old system encouraged employees to drive more miles (eg, over 18,000 you got one-third of the cost as a benefit). Now the benefit is directly related to the greenness of the vehicle.

The Revenue can challenge taxpayers who claim substantial amounts of their mileage as being for business. It is beholden on anyone who thinks the claim is correct to prove their case. That means keeping a detailed log of all car journeys, for business and pleasure – a tedious task for the dubious possibility of gaining a few extra miles from the Revenue.

The taxman might accept a month's log as being representative of the year as a whole. But don't put mileages down in neat round figures – eg, 50, 100 or 250 miles. The Revenue will almost always be suspicious of such laziness.

There is a peculiar rule about motoring expenses to be wary of. When a taxpayer owns and rents out a property, the cost of any journey he makes to collect rent on that property can be set off against his income as an allowable expense. But if he drives to collect the rent and on the way home drops off at Tesco's to do a little shopping, or buys a sandwich from a garage, then the cost of the journey is no longer allowable because of its 'dual purpose'. Parents who buy a house for their children whilst at university cannot claim the cost of the journey to collect rent from their offsprings' flatmates because the journey also (presumably) is made for the purpose of seeing their children.

The Revenue's green policy on transport has been taken to some bizarre extremes. For example, a taxpayer who uses his bicycle for business travel can claim 20p a mile – this is not what most people think of as a business cycle. (No travelling expense to or from work is allowable – not even shoe leather for those who walk to work in what is an even more environmentally friendly manner.) Cyclists get some other extra bonuses too. They get a bike and safety gear that are not saddled with tax. And, six mornings a year, they are allowed to have a tax-free breakfast. When-

ever the Revenue question such claims, taxpayers are usually too tyred to respond.

Termination payments

Employees have to be particularly careful when they leave a company and receive a pay-off at the end of their period of service. The first £30,000 of such a pay-off is tax-free, but if the employee is given their company car

> ### Favourite targets for PAYE enquiries
>
> - Car fuel.
> - Ex-gratia/termination payments.
> - Foreign connections.
> - Entertaining.
> - Excessive travel.
> - Loans in depreciating foreign currencies.
> - Payments in kind, including platinum sponge, wine, carpets, etc.
> - Personal expenditure.
> - Self-employed status.
> - Special awards.
> - Travel to/from home.

as well then that is taxable (at its market value, not its book value).

A long-running case involving a music company helped to establish the difference between end-of-service payments that are contractual and end-of-service payments that are merely compensation for ending the service. The company was making a number of its senior executives redundant and their contract said that the company might pay them in lieu of notice. Their end-of-service payment was thus deemed to be contractual (and taxable). Contracts of employment should never imply that payment will be made in lieu of notice. There has to be 'no expectation to receive it' tax-free on the part of the employee.

Share options

New skirmishes between the taxpayer and the Revenue are starting all the time, and share options have become an increasingly significant battleground in recent years. The amounts involved can be considerable.

It is the duty of the employer to pay PAYE on profits that his employees make on their stock options. He then has 30 days from the time that the option has been exercised to collect the tax from the employee. If he doesn't do it within that time, then the PAYE not made good by the employee is treated as a benefit, and is taxable as such.

Thirty days is a very tight time frame, especially for cases where the taxpayer is an employee of a UK company but has stock options in, for example, the company's US parent. In such a case there is no reason why the UK company should ever know about the exercising of the options by its employee. It is often not in a position to act as a tax collector within 30 months, never mind 30 days.

In effect, this can become a tax on a tax, something that is unacceptable under most countries' fiscal legislation. It is an example of the Revenue's occasional outbursts of dirty warfare.

Other benefits

In another famous skirmish over benefits, a company in the West Country gave its employees 10p coins to enable them to get coffee out of the company's machines. The Revenue said that they would tax the 10p, even though 'light refreshment' as such is not considered a benefit (ie, the coffee and biscuits that an employer provides to its employees in the workplace do not have to appear on the employees' P11D form for recording benefits).

The Revenue, however, took the case of the 10p

pieces to court. And they won. Not surprisingly perhaps, in view of their deep understanding of tax matters, the tabloid newspapers' headlines the next day declared that the 'Inland Revenue taxes coffee'. But that was not the case. The Revenue were taxing the cash, not the coffee. If the company had given tokens that only worked in the coffee machines, then they would have been tax-free.

There is another curious benefits anomaly, this time over mobile phones. If a company provides an employee with a mobile phone and pays for all the calls made on that phone, the user is not considered to have received any taxable benefit – even if virtually all the calls are made for private purposes. (Not that companies are likely to give their employees a mobile phone under such conditions!) If, on the other hand, the employee pays his own mobile-phone bill and gets it reimbursed by the company, then that is a taxable benefit.

The increasingly common practice of lending laptops to a company's employees only gives rise to a taxable benefit in exceptional circumstances. A benefit of less than £500 in any one year is tax-free. As the benefit is calculated as 20 per cent of the higher of the market value or the cost of the computer, the machine has to have been purchased for more than £2,500 to give rise to any taxable benefit, provided no other expenses are paid. It is a very sophisticated machine (or one with some very sophisticated software) that costs so much these days.

Valuation

A common cause of skirmishes of various kinds is the question of valuation. How much a taxable gain or benefit is worth is often not clear-cut. And the Revenue's opinion on the matter can diverge sharply from the taxpayer's.

Valuing shares or share options in private companies, for example, is a particularly thorny issue, and the Revenue have a special department devoted to the task. The market for shares in family firms is purely

There is an almost direct correlation between the elevation of an executive within a corporation and his desire to own a yacht. Some generous companies go so far as to buy boats for their senior executives to enjoy. But don't push the boat out too far, for it can very easily give rise to a taxable charge. The benefit of the vessel is considered to go with its availability, not its use.

So if a yacht is owned by a company and is effectively available at all times to the managing director, then that managing director will be deemed to have benefited in each year to the tune of 20 per cent of the higher of the market value when the yacht was first provided or the cost of the yacht. If the yacht cost £5 million, for example, there is £1 million a year of benefit … not to mention the running costs and the cost of a crew. Neither the managing director nor his captain need ever have set foot on the thing's wretched teak for it to give rise to a taxable benefit on that scale.

The managing director's only sure-fire escape is to charter the vessel. When it is chartered to someone else, then the boat is genuinely not available to the company's executives and cannot therefore give rise to a taxable benefit. Otherwise, the clock's ticking … and the directors may be sinking.

hypothetical if the family has no mind to sell them. So how to ascertain their value for tax purposes?

An important principle about the valuation of benefits was established in 1991 by the case of Pepper v Hart. This established that when a service is provided to an employee, the value of the benefit is the marginal cost, not the full cost. The case involved a schoolmaster who sent his daughter to the private school where he was a teacher. She was allowed to go to the school free and nobody disputed that her father was obtaining a benefit. But the value of that benefit was deemed to be the marginal cost of having an extra pupil at the school, not the average cost (or the fees paid by the other pupils). It made a big difference.

This principle was then applied to airline employees. They are now taxed only on the marginal cost of the free tickets that they and their families are able to enjoy. On a flight where their seats would otherwise have been empty, this is next to nothing.

The valuation of benefits is not always so favourable to the taxpayer, however. When company assets (such as cars) are given to executives, the benefit is not the value of the car as recorded in the company's books (usually a very low figure), but the full market value of the vehicle.

Indeed, the valuation rules can sometimes work cruelly against the taxpayer. In a recent case, a taxpayer exercised his options in a telecoms company and gave rise to a tax liability on the gain – 40 per cent of £x million. By the time he came to pay the tax, however, the value of his shares had fallen below the tax liability – ie, they were worth less than £0.4x million. Selling the shares was then not enough to pay the tax that was due on them.

There is a feeling that the Revenue will try to introduce legislation to modify the tax charge in such circumstances. But it will be too late for the guy with shares in the telecoms company. Tax legislation is rarely retrospective and, so far, never to the taxpayer's benefit.

Capital gains

Since self-assessment was first introduced, the tax-return form has been considerably revised. In particular, the return has been altered to encourage the taxpayer to give more information about capital gains. There are now eight pages devoted to capital gains (more than for any other section of the form), where there used to be only two.

Whereas a taxpayer's income is relatively smooth year on year (even, surprisingly, the income of the self-employed), capital gains tend to come in big one-off blobs, and these tend to flash warning signals all over the Revenue's computers.

The whole area of capital-gains tax is a minefield for the unwary. Those who do not take great care of their assets can find big chunks of wealth blown to smithereens by the tax. It is almost always wise for taxpayers who are about to realise a large capital gain to seek professional advice. The rules on what is and what is not taxable are very complicated.

For the purposes of this book, it is enough to know that everyone is entitled to a tax-free capital gain of £7,500 a year. This is one of several areas of tax law that is prejudiced against the unmarried. For married people the limit is, in effect, £15,000 because spouses can shuffle their assets around before a sale so that each gains £7,500 tax-free.

Trusts

If anything is more complicated (and more of a minefield for taxpayers) than capital gains it is trusts. For a long time trusts have been used as a means to shelter income and capital gains from tax. So, for the Revenue, the sighting of a trust on the horizon is almost automatically suspicious. If an inspector can prove that the sole purpose of a trust is to avoid tax and that the trust is no more than a

---

Some valid reasons for setting up a trust

- To hold property on behalf of minors who cannot legally hold property in their own name.
- To enable one beneficiary to enjoy income, but for the underlying capital to be retained for others.
- To protect capital which may otherwise be dissipated.
- To achieve tax-efficient maintenance of grandchildren (eg, school fees).
- As a way of passing on a family home.
- To make a gift and leaseback of assets at full market rent.
- For parking CGT losses.
- For social reasons. To have something to brag about at the golf club.

sham, he can take the taxpayer to court to get the trust rendered null and void for tax purposes.

Trustees of any trust are obliged to give the Revenue a report each year of the exact amount of income that has been paid to the trust's beneficiaries during the year, and the amount of tax that has been withheld on that income.

With offshore trusts which have UK beneficiaries, there is no such obligation. But the Revenue inform the trustees of such trusts that if they do not fill in a return they (the Revenue) may feel strangely compelled to carry out an enquiry into the tax affairs of all of the trust's UK beneficiaries.

Overseas

Enquiries into a taxpayer's overseas affairs can be gruelling. In the first place, they can take for ever. Getting overseas banks, for instance, to certify interest or dividend

payments can be like pulling teeth from a rhino. In the second place, the word 'overseas' is like a red rag to a bull for the Revenue. They will, for example, look very carefully at taxpayers with overseas income on which they are claiming relief for foreign tax. Such reliefs are governed by a network of double-taxation agreements between the UK and other countries.

The Revenue dislike the word 'overseas' because there are so many opportunities to avoid tax for people who either have an income abroad or who are themselves not entirely British. The best opportunity comes from a taxpayer's 'domicile'. People who can claim that they are not domiciled in this country (even though they are resident here) are taxed only on the amount of their earnings in the rest of the world which they remit to this country. In terms of tax strategy, this is a no-brainer. It doesn't take von Clausewitz

The 18th-century Prussian general Carl von Clausewitz was one of the greatest military strategists ever to have lived. One of his most famous sayings was: 'No one starts a war – or rather, no one in his senses ought to do so – without first being clear in his mind what he intends to achieve by that war and how he intends to conduct it.' Taxpayers, take note.

to show that it gives taxpayers an almost assured victory over the Revenue.

The rules on domicile (when you are and when you aren't, and what benefits you get when you aren't) are peculiar. For example, as far as inheritance tax is concerned, people become domiciled in the UK once they have been resident here for 17 out of the past 20 years. But for the purposes of income tax and capital-gains tax, they can remain non-domiciled for the whole of their life. There are even cases where the children of

non-domiciled parents have established non-domiciled status even when they have been born in the UK and spent most of their lives in the country.

Domicile is usually established in the first year of a new arrival's residence in this country. Residents fill in a form, known as a 'Dom One', on which they list their 'business, personal, social or other connections' with their country of birth. They also have to state that they do not intend to stay permanently in the UK (and certainly not after their death).

The standard tax return asks taxpayers to certify that their domicile position has been considered during the past six years. But even after six years there is not much the Revenue can do to change that position if the taxpayer's fundamental long-term view of his life has not changed. This is in contrast to the tax system in the United States where all residents (and, indeed, all passport holders) are taxed on their worldwide income and capital gains regardless of where it arises and of where they want to be buried.

But watch this space. There is now much talk of abolishing the domicile system, which in effect makes Britain a generous tax haven for rich foreigners, and the Revenue are at the moment preparing a consultation document on the subject.

The other important idea here is that of residence. A taxpayer's residence in the UK is established by the number of days spent in the country in any given tax year.

Anyone resident and domiciled in the UK is liable to tax on their worldwide income, just like an American taxpayer. There are special rules for people like airline pilots and air hostesses, however, who spend much of their time working in the air, resident (in effect) in no man's land.

In this day and age, when passports are rarely stamped for travellers going from one EU country to another, it is not as easy for the Revenue to demonstrate that taxpayers have failed to observe the non-residence rules. However, the names of all passengers passing through airports, for example, are preserved for years. And credit-card and telephone bills invariably tell a story of their own. One non-resident claims that he always comes back to the UK on the Eurostar train (inside it, not underneath it) because he knows that passports are never stamped on the cross-Channel trip.

Smaller skirmishes

The big battles between taxpayers and the Revenue are raging more or less continuously. But from time to time the Revenue get a particular bee in their bonnet, taking upon themselves to battle against a small battalion on a seemingly narrow front for no apparent reason. Once, for example, it was the turn of taxi-drivers to come under close inspection. Then doctors, dentists and other professionals were subjected to the third degree.

Right now, the Revenue seem to have taken against waiters in restaurants and also (rather more boldly) against bouncers at night clubs. A London district office recently carried out a survey of bouncers to see if they were wrongly claiming to be self-employed.

Waiters are in the inspectors' eye because of the 'tronc' system, the method by which tips are handed out to staff. Even if these cash payments are declared in full by the recipient (and so subjected to the right amount of tax) they avoid the National Insurance net.

And it is not as if they are too small to bother about. In one case, restaurants were paying their waiters £100 a week, but guaranteeing them an additional £150 a week from the tronc. At top London restaurants, waiters can pick up more than three times their wages in tips.

In a case involving a group of 12 Chinese restaurants, the individual managers within each restaurant were supposed to manage the tronc system for their establishment. The company offered to do the job for them, but wanted to take an administrative charge out of the total pool. The Revenue argued that this tainted the tronc, putting it somehow into the control of the company, and thereby making it subject to National Insurance.

One small group of tax inspectors has been instructed to look only at professional football clubs and their players, and the extent to which they might be avoiding tax. A test case involving a top England player is trying to establish whether the payment by his club of

a sum for his 'image rights' – for example, the money paid for allowing his face to appear on the back of a T-shirt – can be separated from his regular salary. If it can, then the club is free to pay it into a separate company, and it can be treated separately for tax purposes. The Revenue have already tried unsuccessfully (in 1995) to challenge payments for image rights that were paid into the personal companies of two other prominent players. An own goal perhaps.

The spoils of war

Penalties and fines

There are no excuses for the late delivery of statutory forms, other than 'I'm dead', and even that might not work since the responsibility may well devolve onto the dead person's executors. In this respect at least it is unlike warfare. There 'I'm dead' is genuinely final.

The system of fines and penalties can become extremely complicated. For the purposes of this book, it is enough to understand a few of the basic principles. The Revenue are less strict than the VAT office in imposing fines for lateness, but they are getting stricter. The basic fine for not sending in your return on time (ie, before the end of January) is £100. The Revenue have said that almost a million people (out of the nine million taxpayers who fill in a return) miss this deadline. This should bring in fines of £100 million – not bad for doing nothing.

But it is not enough for the Revenue. They have

said that of the one million late filers, some 400,000 have still not submitted their returns by the end of July. These laggards they are proposing in future to fine at the rate of £60 a day, bringing in (in theory) £24 million every day. The Revenue say that a couple of pilot schemes have shown this to be 'an extraordinarily effective way' to accelerate the filing of returns. Hardly surprising.

If you make a simple error – forgetting to sign the form at the end, for example, or ticking a box saying that something is attached, and it isn't – the Revenue will return the form and give you 14 days to correct the mistake. If you keep within that schedule there will be no penalty.

There are also surcharges for not paying tax on time. The basic surcharge is 5 per cent of the amount of tax outstanding. If there is some tax still unpaid six months later (ie, by the end of July) then there is another 5 per cent surcharge. In addition, interest is charged on the unpaid tax. It starts clocking up from the date that the tax is due.

The amounts paid to the Revenue in penalties and surcharges have rocketed in recent years. In 1994, before self-assessment when there were no surcharges, the amount paid in penalties was just under £2 million. In 2000, penalties of over £63 million were paid, and surcharges of over £50 million.

Filing a tax return electronically can speed things up

In America, penalties of up to 20 per cent can be imposed for 'a substantial understatement of tax'. An understatement is considered to be substantial if it is more than the greater of:

- 10 per cent of the tax required to be shown on the return; or
- $5,000.

It is the complete opposite of the rules for tipping in restaurants – where anything less than 10 per cent is totally unacceptable.

since the Revenue send an electronic reply the following day to confirm that the filing has been received. The downside to this method is that it can take an age to download the Revenue's electronic form (to be found on www.inlandrevenue.gov.uk), unless you have a very powerful computer. In practice, confidentiality is also still a problem, and the system is not proving popular. At the moment, fewer than 1 per cent of taxpayers file their returns via the Internet.

In America, the electronic filing of tax returns has become almost commonplace, and there are a number of software packages on the market to help the taxpayer to fill in his e-return. Such practice is sure to spread to the UK before long.

A taxpayer who is discovered to have been concealing income from the tax inspector (or fraudulently inflating his expenses) is in a completely different ball-park as far as penalties are concerned. In such cases the penalty can rise as high as 100 per cent of the tax due. But it very rarely reaches that level. The highest that is imposed (unless the circumstances are truly exceptional) is 20 per cent. Such penalties do not apply where the errors in a taxpayer's return were perpetrated innocently.

All tax penalties can be mitigated through negotiation. The Revenue have considerable discretion here. They can even waive the fines and penalties altogether if they have a mind to.

Three things are taken into account when the Revenue are considering mitigation:

1. The gravity of the offence; here the inspector can reduce the penalty by up to 40 per cent.
2. The degree of co-operation by the taxpayer; here again the inspector can reduce the penalty by up to 40 per cent.
3. The extent to which the taxpayer volunteers that a mistake has been made. The Revenue can reduce the penalty by up to a further 20 per cent for full and early disclosure. Clearly, if all these possibilities are exercised, the taxpayer may end up getting off scot free – ie, only paying the tax that was in any case due.

A recent European Court of Human Rights ruling confirmed that penalties cannot be imposed on the living in respect of acts committed by a person now deceased.

The Revenue are not keen on prosecution. They do prosecute, especially where the taxpayer has 'created' something – false invoices or backdated documents, for example. But one unexceptional tax adviser has come across only two clients who have been prosecuted in 15 years' experience.

At the moment, the government is far more eager to punish 'benefits snitches' than tax evaders. Where

the Revenue come across workers who are being paid cash in brown envelopes (for some sort of casual labour) at the same time as they are claiming benefits (for unemployment or the like), there is a very high chance of prosecution. But the prosecuting body will probably be the relevant benefits office, not the Revenue themselves.

The Revenue usually prosecute people for the common-law crime of 'cheat'. It sounds much more offensive than 'fraud'. Nobody wants to be branded a cheat; being called a fraudster is not such a disgrace.

In a recent six-month period, the Revenue issued only three press notices about prosecutions. They were headed:

- 'Tax credit cheat sentenced to community service'.
- 'Unqualified accountant sentenced to 12 months for cheating'.
- 'Tax cheat barrister loses appeal against jail sentence.'

It is worth noting that the harshest sentences are meted out to those who are assumed to know better – accountants, lawyers and the like. The accountant and the barrister in the examples above both got jail sentences; the third subject of prosecution was sentenced to community service only. Although the tax barrister was convicted of cheating for his own account, rather than being involved in the cheating of his clients, it did not help his case (or his sentencing – he got four and a half years) that he was a member of the bar.

Collection

In order to collect unpaid tax, inspectors can seize an individual taxpayer's assets. They do not need to call on a bailiff. They issue what is known as a 'walk-in possession order' and come and take goods to the value of the unpaid tax.

There are certain assets, however, that they cannot touch. These include the tools of a person's trade, the basic necessities of life, and perishable goods. Into the last category comes food, including frozen food. And since frozen food cannot be taken, neither can the freezer.

Raids undertaken by the Revenue to seize assets are rare. In almost 15 years service with the Revenue, one inspector went on only one raid. It was of a small company that supposedly had no presence in the UK – all its business was allegedly offshore. In its case, the Revenue seized everything from the company's 'non-existent' premises, down to the telephone directories and the secretaries' diaries.

The end of the engagement

The only way that an enquiry can be brought to a formal end is by the issuance of a closure notice. This is a standard letter from the Revenue saying that their enquiry is being closed down for good. In it, the inspector states the amount of tax that he believes ought to have been paid according to his amendment of the self-assessment tax return. The letter may make suggestions as to how the taxpayer can keep better records so that the same mistakes are not made again in the future. It assumes that

Local district enquiries

Nine steps from start to finish – a typical investigation

1   **Notification letter from the tax district, or voluntary disclosure (issue of Section 9A TMA 1970 notice)**

An investigation is prompted when the tax district believes that information supplied on a tax return is incorrect; or that more information is required to understand the disclosure made; or if the taxpayer has been selected for a random enquiry; or if the taxpayer volunteers information.

2   **Appointment of advisers**

If an unrepresented taxpayer receives notification that an enquiry is to be launched by the Revenue, they should appoint a team of professional advisers.

3   **Establish the facts and obtain information**

The letter explaining the detail of the enquiry should be carefully reviewed and the documentation requested be identified. If the documents are not held by the agent, they should be requested from either the client or relevant third parties. It is also good practice to estimate whether any deadline for the submission of the documents to the Revenue can be met, and if not write to the inspector stating the date by which the information is expected to be available.

4   **Manage the taxpayer**

The professional adviser should explain to the taxpayer why the Revenue have asked for additional data and what action is being taken to respond to the queries raised. Advise the taxpayer of potential tax at stake.

5   **Agree response**

Once all data is available to respond to the Revenue, the client should be invited to comment upon and approve a draft letter written by the professional adviser to the inspector. Once agreement has been reached – perhaps after a meeting between the adviser and the client – the letter is submitted to the inspector.

6   **Obtain Revenue agreement**
Once the inspector has received the adviser's letter/report, a follow-up timetable implemented by the adviser should ensure that agreement is reached swiftly. Alternatively, if additional information is required by the inspector, a deadline should be proposed for this.

7   **Clarification meeting**
In some cases, particularly if the enquiry is not an aspect enquiry (see page 14), the inspector may wish to meet the adviser to discuss certain issues. This will usually focus more on the areas of perceived 'risk' where the tax at stake merits more detailed examination and/or clarification.

8   **Closure notice (s28A (1) & (2) TMA 1970)**
Once the inspector is in a position to close the enquiry, a closure notice will be issued to the taxpayer, with the adviser being sent a copy. This will summarise what amendments the inspector has made to the taxpayer's self-assessment. This s28A notice will also state that any tax payable as a result of the amendment must be paid within 30 days of the issue date.

Alternatively, an appeal against the inspector's revised self-assessment should be lodged, again within 30 days. The appeal should be in writing and should state the grounds for the appeal.

9   **Final step**
Provided the content of the s28A notice is agreed, the taxpayer should pay any additional tax due with the 30-day period.

if the taxpayer does not reply within 30 days, then he has agreed with the letter and that's the end of it.

> One accountant included the word 'allegedly'
> 18 times in a one-page offer document. He alleges
> that this is a world record.

The closing of an enquiry is a bit like the end of a trial. A taxpayer cannot be quizzed about the same things twice. No self-assessment form can be the subject of more than one enquiry. If a taxpayer does not agree to end the enquiry (perhaps he disputes the Revenue's valuation of a particular asset) then his only resort is to the tax commissioners (see page 42).

On the other hand, at any stage during an enquiry a taxpayer can apply to the commissioners and ask them to issue an order commanding the tax inspector to close the enquiry within a specified period of time. It is a statutory requirement that the commissioners find in the taxpayer's favour unless the inspector has reasonable grounds for keeping the enquiry open. The taxpayer and/or his representative has the right to attend the commissioners' hearings. Either side can appeal against the commissioners' ruling, and the matter then comes before a court.

In one case, an inspector wrote to a taxpayer saying that he did not agree with the taxpayer's figures, but he was closing the case anyway. Such peremptory haste suggests that he had a personal target to meet, and that he was a bit behind. In any case, he reserved the right to reopen the enquiry later should he so wish.

> 'The enemy came. He was beaten. I am tired. Good night.'
>
> *The Vicomte de Turenne after the Battle of Tunen, June 14th 1658.*

The Revenue do win many of their skirmishes with taxpayers. To date, however, there is no way of telling whether they are winning the war or not. There are few meaningful statistics on the outcome of enquiries under the new rules on self-assessment.

What is known is that many enquiries are an unmitigated disaster for the taxpayer who is the subject of the enquiry. They disrupt their business life and their private life, leading at the extreme to bankruptcy and divorce. After an enquiry, taxpayers invariably vow that they will do everything they can to avoid going through such an experience again.

After the first world war, Woodrow Wilson, president of the United States, said: 'The war we have been through, though it was shot through with terror, is not to be compared with the war we will have to face next time.' Revenue enquiries will continue, but none will ever be exactly the same as those that have gone before.

War or Peace